W9-ASU-286

Laze in the Comfortable Kingdom of
LIONS

599
L10

Published by Wildlife Education, Ltd.

12233 Thatcher Court, Poway, California 92064

contact us at: **1-800-477-5034**

e-mail us at: **animals@zoobooks.com**

visit us at: **www.zoobooks.com**

ISBN 0-937934-81-X

Lions

Created and Written by
John Bonnett Wexo

Scientific Consultants
Michael R. Worley, D.V.M.
Zoological Society of San Diego

Christopher A. Shaw
Eric Scott
George C. Page Museum

Art Credits

All paintings by Richard Orr

Photographic Credits

On the Cover: An African Lion Cub

Contents

*L*ions have been admired and feared by people for thousands of years. Ancient hunters sometimes found themselves competing with lions when they hunted, and the greater strength and size of the lions usually meant that the cats got the prey and the humans did not. It was also true that the lions could easily kill people. For these reasons, people developed the two main human attitudes about lions that have survived to this day: admiration and fear.

When we look at lions today, we can't help but admire them. We still feel a thrill because they are so strong and so powerful. We marvel at their great skill in hunting, and the easy grace they display when they move. At the same time, we may feel unhappy and fearful about the fact that lions kill prey. Lions are *predators*—animals that hunt other animals. The life of a lion is focused on the chasing, catching and eating of prey. This shocks some people, but we must understand that lions have no choice about the matter. Unlike humans, they have only one way to survive. They must hunt to stay alive. If a lion stops hunting, it will die.

Beyond this, lions may actually help other groups of animals when they hunt. If predators do not kill some of the prey animals, the numbers of those animals soon grow too large for the amount of food available to them. In some places, humans have killed all or most of the predators, and the results have been horrible. In these cases, the numbers of prey animals have skyrocketed, and without enough food to feed them all, thousands of prey animals have starved to death. In nature, predators like lions take just enough prey animals to keep the numbers of those animals in *balance* with the food supply.

Lions are members of a group called *big cats*, and the lion is one of the biggest cats in the world. This group includes other big predators—tigers, leopards, and jaguars, with the Siberian tiger being the only cat larger than the lion. But lions are different from most other cats in that they live in groups. They hunt together, guard their territory together, and raise their young together. Lions that live in groups can catch more food than a single lion can. And they can protect themselves better. Lions that are born into groups have larger families to care for them.

As you will see on the following pages, lions are native today to only two parts of the world, Africa and India. In the past, however, there were lions *all over the world*.

In the past, lions lived all over the world, on every continent but Antarctica and Australia. But today, they are only found in parts of Africa and a small area of India. (The green areas on the map show where lions lived in the past. The red areas show where they live today.)

Eight thousand years ago, there were lions in North and South America. As recently as 2,000 years ago, there were still lions in parts of Europe. And only 200 years ago, the ranges of lions in Africa and India were much larger.

What happened to all of the lions that used to live in North America and South America? Where did the lions go that used to live in Europe? Why are there so many places in Africa and India where lions can no longer be found? Can you guess what might have happened to them?

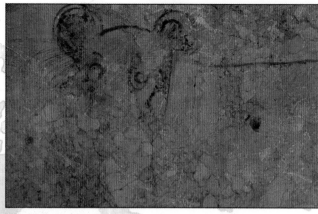

When lions lived in Europe, they were hunted by human hunters. More than 15,000 years ago, this picture of a lion was painted on the wall of a cave in France, probably by hunters. Can you see the rounded lion ears in the painting?

NORTH AMERICA

The last lions in North America disappeared about 8,000 years ago—shortly after the first human hunters appeared on the continent.

NORTH AMERICAN LION
Panthera leo atrox
(Extinct)

Long ago, lions in North America hunted big animals as they do today in Africa. They were the only predators large enough to take down a huge bison.

North American lions were larger than today's lions. Some of them were 12 feet long. Their heads alone were a foot and a half long, and their sharp canine teeth were almost three inches long.

SOUTH AMERICA

AFRICAN LION
Panthera leo
(Living)

EUROPEAN CAVE LION
Panthera leo spelaea
(Extinct)

AFRICAN LION
Panthera leo
(Living)

EUROPE

ASIA

AFRICA

When lions lived in Europe, the climate was much colder than it is today. The lions were larger than lions living today and probably had thick, furry coats to protect them from the cold. Ancient European lions are often called "cave" lions because so many of their skulls have been found in caves that were inhabited by human hunters.

Hundreds of thousands of lions once lived in Asia. Today, there are about 330 left, living in a small protected area called the Gir Forest and in the neighboring Barda Forest in India.

There were once millions of lions everywhere in Africa except the Sahara Desert. As human populations in Africa have increased, lions have been driven out of many areas where they once lived to make room for human cities, ranches, and farms. Hunters also killed many lions. Today, there are fewer than 200,000 lions in all of Africa.

ASIATIC LION
Panthera leo persica
(Living)

9

Only adult male lions have manes. A large, bushy mane makes a male look even bigger than he is. This helps to attract females and scare away other males. The mane may also protect a lion's face and neck when he fights with other males.

Lions must hunt to live, and they are wonderful hunters. Their bodies are almost perfectly made for catching prey. They have excellent *eyes and ears* to help them find prey. *Strong muscles* help them chase and bring down even large animals. And they have *special teeth* for holding and eating the animals they catch.

Lions have the biggest eyes of any meat-eating animal, and can sometimes see prey that is miles away. Like other cats, they can see very well in the dark—and this helps them to hunt at night. (Many lions do most of their hunting at night.) The ears of a lion also help to find prey. A lion can sometimes hear animals that are more than a mile away.

When they hunt, lions can run fast for short distances to catch prey. But many times, they prefer to *sneak up* on the animals they are hunting. Very slowly, a lion creeps as close as it can get without being seen. Then, when the prey animal is looking the other way, the lion leaps! A lion can jump as much as 35 feet in one leap.

Lions have long, sharp teeth for catching and holding prey. These teeth are called *canines*. Can you find them below?

A lion's strong claws are used to grab and hold prey.

When you go to the zoo, you will see that lions keep turning their ears in many different directions. By doing this, they can hear sounds from many directions. In tall grass, lions may not be able to see prey, but they can *hear* it.

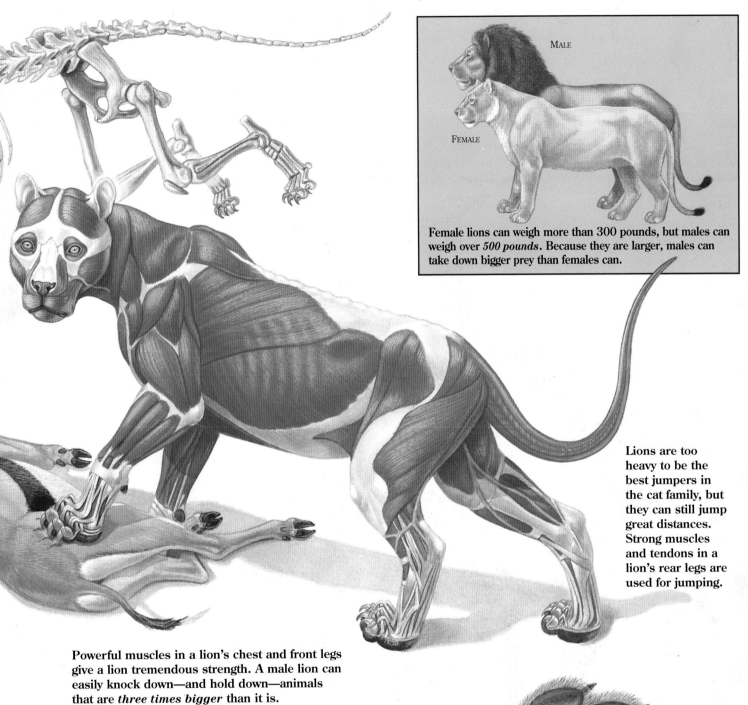

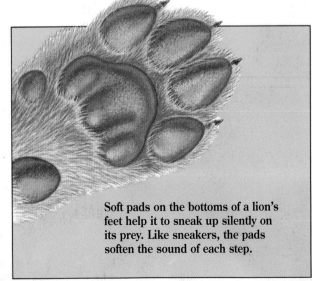

Female lions can weigh more than 300 pounds, but males can weigh over *500 pounds*. Because they are larger, males can take down bigger prey than females can.

Lions are too heavy to be the best jumpers in the cat family, but they can still jump great distances. Strong muscles and tendons in a lion's rear legs are used for jumping.

Powerful muscles in a lion's chest and front legs give a lion tremendous strength. A male lion can easily knock down—and hold down—animals that are *three times bigger* than it is.

In addition to their canine teeth, lions have sharp cutting teeth for slicing up their food. These are called carnassial (kar-**nass**-ee-uhl) teeth, and are located behind the canine teeth. Can you find the carnassial teeth on the lion at left? The small teeth at the front of the mouth nip small pieces of meat off bones. A lion's tongue has a very rough surface for scraping the last tiny bits of meat off bones.

Soft pads on the bottoms of a lion's feet help it to sneak up silently on its prey. Like sneakers, the pads soften the sound of each step.

13

Family life is very important to lions. Of all the cats in the world, they are *the only ones* that live together in large family groups. Other cats, like leopards and tigers, live alone most of the time. But lions believe in *togetherness*. They raise their young together, and they hunt together.

A family of lions is called a *pride*. There are between 3 and 40 lions in a pride—and a typical pride includes a group of females, their young, and several males. The females are usually sisters or closely related, and they often stay with the same pride all of their lives. But the male lions usually stay with a pride for only a few years. Eventually, invading males try to take over the pride, and a battle takes place between the pride males and the invaders. The outcome is shown below.

The lions in a pride are usually very friendly with each other. Often, when they meet each other, they rub their heads together in a friendly greeting.

The main job of male lions is to protect the *territory* of the pride, the area in which the pride lives. From time to time, other males may enter the territory and challenge the lions that live there **1**.

Often, a savage fight takes place between the pride males and the males from outside **2**. Sometimes, they fight so violently that one or more of the males is seriously injured or even killed.

2

1

OUTSIDER CHALLENGES MALE IN PRIDE

The loud roar of a lion has several uses. When they are hunting at night or can't see each other during the day, the lions in a pride sometimes roar to keep in touch. Males often roar to chase away intruders into the pride's territory.

AFRAID

ANNOYED

Because they live so closely together, lions in a pride need good ways to communicate their emotions to each other. They have expressive faces to help them do it. Can you tell what emotions these lions are communicating?

ANGRY

4

DEFEATED MALE LEAVES

If the pride lions win, they get to stay with the pride. If the lions from outside win, they take over the pride **3**, and the defeated males have to go away **4**.

Male lions mostly watch for marauders and sleep. The females usually do the hunting. When the hunt is over, the males often drive the females away from the meat and take "the lion's share" for themselves. The females and cubs eat the rest.

3

NEW MALE JOINS PRIDE

The lions of a pride enjoy doing everything together. Even when they sleep, they usually stay close together, sometimes even lying on top of one another. Lions love to sleep. When their stomachs are full, they may spend 20 hours every day just lying around, resting and sleeping.

Getting food isn't easy. Lions are expert hunters, but they often have to work hard to get their food. *Working together* makes hunting easier, and this is one major reason why lions live in prides. A group of lions hunting together can catch more food than a single lion hunting alone.

The females do almost all of the hunting. They sometimes use an amazing system of teamwork to catch prey, as you will see below.

As strong as female lions are, prey animals that weigh more than 650 pounds are usually too big for them to catch. The greater size and strength of male lions is necessary to bring down huge animals like the Cape buffalo, or even some large zebras.

When females hunt together, they start by dividing into two groups. One group circles around to hide ahead of the prey **1**.

After the first group is in position, the other lions show themselves and chase the prey toward the first group **2**.

If everything works out, the prey runs right into the waiting lions of the first group **3**.

Because hunting can be such hard work, lions always appreciate a free meal if they can get it. When they see other predators catching prey, lions will steal it, if possible. And usually it's *very* possible—because most animals don't really want to argue with a pack of hungry lions!

When their usual prey is hard to find, lions will sometimes eat the most surprising things. In hard times, lions have been known to eat porcupines, fish, snakes, turtles, locusts, termites, peanuts, fruit—and even *rotten wood*.

No matter how hard they try, lions simply can't catch most of the animals they go after. Females hunting together can catch only about two out of every five animals they hunt. A lion hunting alone can catch only about *one* out of every six animals that it chases. Lions sometimes go hungry for days.

Young lions are **well protected** from the moment they are born. And they need all the protection they can get. At the moment of their births, they are almost totally helpless. They may weigh less than three pounds and can hardly crawl. Sometimes, their eyes don't even open until they are five or six days old.

The babies are called *cubs*. Unlike adult lions, cubs have spots on their coats (as shown below). Many people believe that the spots help to protect the cubs by making it harder for predators to see them.

But the greatest protection for a young lion comes from its mother and the other females in the pride. *All* of the females work together to protect and feed all of the cubs in the pride. And because the females in a pride can catch more food than a single mother could catch, all of the babies eat better and stay healthier. You might say that a young lion has *many mothers* to love it and keep it safe.

A mother lion usually keeps her cubs hidden for the first few weeks of their lives, in a safe place away from the pride. Then she brings them out and introduces them to the rest of the "family." When the cubs are young, their mother carries them around in the same way that house cats carry their kittens—she picks them up with her teeth, holding them gently by their necks.

Lion cubs are born in groups called *litters*. Usually, there are three cubs in a litter. But sometimes there are as many as five.

Like kittens, cubs are born with an instinct to hunt. Almost as soon as they can walk, they start pouncing on anything that moves. In this way, they begin to learn the skills they will need to catch their food.

When mother lions go out to hunt, the cubs must stay behind. If some females are not hunting, they will take care of the cubs. But if all of the pride's females go hunting, the cubs are hidden in tall grass or among rocks to protect them from predators.

Male lions are fierce creatures, but they can be remarkably gentle with cubs. At times, big males will even let cubs tug at their manes or play with their tails.

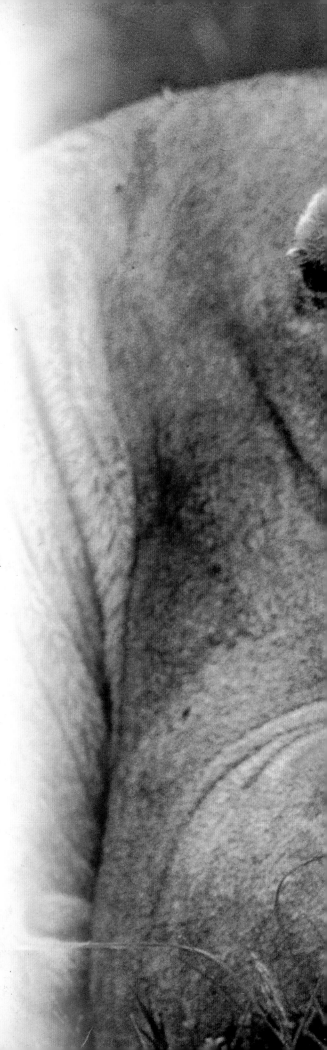

The future of lions is in the hands of human beings. In the past, human hunters were responsible for the extinction of lions in many parts of the world. Until recently, hunters played a big role in destroying lions in Africa and India, the last two places where lions have survived. But today, that has changed. Hunters are no longer a major threat to lions—it is *builders and farmers* who are the greatest danger.

Early human hunters in Africa were armed only with spears, and the number of lions they could kill was limited. Then people arrived from Europe with guns, and the killing of lions became much easier. In North Africa, lions were wiped out entirely. In other parts of Africa, it looked as though lions would soon become totally extinct.

Just in time, some good people acted to save the lions. They worked to have *safe areas* set aside—game preserves and national parks in which lions were sometimes fully protected from humans with guns. Today, most of the lions in Africa and all of the lions in India live in protected areas.

But now there is a new problem. The number of people in Africa and India grows so fast that protected areas are in danger.

Lions need *three things* to stay alive. They must have a *territory* in which to hunt, *enough prey* to catch and eat, and *safety from humans*. The growing number of humans in Africa and India could deprive lions of these basic necessities and lead to their extinction.

More people require more food and more living space. As the human population grows, all of the land outside national parks and other safe areas may be taken over for farms and houses. Sooner or later, the only land left for people to take may be inside the national parks and safe areas where lions and other wildlife live.

If this land is taken, lions will be hurt in three ways. With less land, there will be *less space* for lions, and so there will be fewer lions. When people convert wild land into villages and farms, many of the larger plant-eating wild animals are driven out. With fewer prey animals, lions will have *less food*. Finally, when humans replace wild animals with domestic animals like cows and sheep, and the lions have no other prey, the lions will start eating cows and sheep. And *people will start shooting lions again* to protect their livestock.

The way to keep lions on earth is to make sure that national parks and other safe areas in Africa and India are protected and maintained. If we can manage to do this, then lions will be with us for a long time to come.

Index